Legal Disclaimer

Published by Independently Published with ISBN:9798866621637.

The Artificial Candidate

Generative AI and the Future of US Election

Yassine Aqejjaj

Content

Dedication

To Eva,

My love, my life, my light

Foreword

In "The Artificial Candidate: Generative AI and the Future of US Elections," I explore the dynamic interplay between artificial intelligence and the democratic process. Drawing from my deep involvement in the AI field, this book is an endeavor to shed light on how these advanced technologies are reshaping our political landscape.

This work delves into the dual nature of AI within the realm of politics. It is an exploration of how AI, with its vast potential, can both enhance and challenge the democratic process. The book navigates the complex ethical and societal implications of AI in politics, emphasizing the balance between harnessing its power for public good and safeguarding democratic integrity.

Central to the theme is the idea that the tools we develop in the realm of AI can either strengthen the foundations of democracy or undermine them. As we approach a technologically unprecedented election, the need for a critical examination of AI's role in our political systems has never been more pressing.

With "The Artificial Candidate," my goal is to ignite a crucial conversation about the responsible integration of AI in politics. It is a call to thoughtfully consider how this technology can be employed to reinforce, not diminish, the principles of democracy.

Yassine Aqejjaj

The Digital Tempest

The turn of the 21st century bore witness to an unprecedented convergence of technology and politics, culminating in an event that would fundamentally reshape the electoral landscape. The Cambridge Analytica scandal, a saga that unfurled the intrigue of a spy novel, was not merely a breach of digital privacy. It became a testament to the power of data as the new currency of political influence, marking the dawn of an era where information was not just king—it was the kingmaker.

This book begins at this critical inflection point, dissecting the complex narrative that Cambridge Analytica brought to light. It was a revelation that transformed innocent online interactions into a trove of insights, ripe for the taking. This was not the mere collection of data but the intricate mapping of human psyches, where millions of digital personas were distilled into actionable strategies, potent enough to sway the tides of public opinion.

At the epicenter of this storm stood a firm that leveraged "behavioral microtargeting" with a prowess previously unseen. They wielded algorithms like a maestro conducts an orchestra, each movement resonating with an individual's inclinations and biases, each note calibrated to subtly influence the electoral symphony. The repercussions of this scandal reverberated across the globe, igniting a fervent discourse on the sanctity of the democratic process in the digital age.

In the wake of these revelations, this introduction serves not as a call to arms but as an invitation to understanding. We embark on an exploration into the nascent domain of Generative AI—a realm where the creation of digital content by intelligent algorithms is poised to redefine political communication. In this new epoch, AI is the artisan of perception, the sculptor of narrative, capable of swaying public discourse with unprecedented precision.

This juncture, marked by the shadow of Cambridge Analytica, signals the advent of a transformative force in politics. Here, within "The Artificial Candidate," we will traverse the intricate pathways of Generative AI. We will examine the algorithms that are shaping to become the draftsmen of the next viral political manifesto, the architects of synthetic charisma that could one day replace flesh-and-blood candidates, and the arbiters of a new digital authenticity that challenges our conventional wisdom.

Our journey will take us through the corridors of power, illuminated by the glow of screens, where AI's potential to fabricate realities is both a promise and a peril. This chronicle is a mosaic of insights for the electorate, a compendium of foresight for policymakers, and a manifesto for technologists who stand at the crossroads, deciding the direction in which this powerful technology should tread.

As we embark on this expedition, "The Artificial Candidate" invites you to engage with the essential questions at the heart of Generative AI's integration into the political arena. It is a narrative that calls for discernment, for dialogue, and for the deliberate shaping of a future that synergizes technology with the foundational tenets of democracy.

Let us step into this exploration with eyes wide open, ready to confront the challenges and seize the opportunities that lie ahead in the uncharted territory of AI and elections. The Cambridge Analytica scandal was a watershed, not for the data that was exploited, but for the curtain it pulled back, revealing a stage set for the entrance of AI into the political sphere. It was a scandal that forced us to recognize our vulnerabilities in a digitally interconnected world and challenged us to think critically about the nature of influence and the power of data-driven persuasion.

In these pages, we will delve into the ethical quagmires presented by this new technology, the legal battles being fought over its use and misuse, and the societal shifts it may herald. We will meet the thinkers and innovators at AI's cutting edge, the strategists harnessing it for campaign victories, and the activists advocating for its responsible use. We will explore the potential of AI to revitalize civic engagement, to personalize political platforms to individual needs, and to create a more informed and active electorate.

Yet, we will also confront the darker potentials of this technology—the ways in which AI could deepen divides, erode trust in public discourse, and give rise to new forms of manipulation that target not just our preferences but our very perception of reality. We will probe the vulnerabilities of democratic institutions facing the onslaught of AI-generated content, seeking answers to the pressing question of how to preserve the integrity of our elections in the face of these powerful new tools.

This book aims to serve as a beacon, a guide through the tumultuous seas of political change. It is for the voter who casts their ballot with hope for the future, for the policymaker balancing the scales of progress and protection, and for the reader who seeks to understand the forces shaping the world of tomorrow. As we turn each page, let us consider how the lessons of the past can inform our steps into the future, guiding us towards a horizon where technology empowers democracy to flourish in new and exciting ways.

Chapter 1

The AI Genesis in Politics

In the grand theater of political strategy, the emergence of Generative Artificial Intelligence (AI) marks a profound shift, akin to the introduction of the printing press—an innovation that would redefine the dissemination of information and the very mechanics of influence. This chapter seeks to place Generative AI within the vast tapestry of political evolution, tracing its lineage from the earliest methods of data analysis to its current role as a pivotal instrument in the political arena.

Generative AI: The New Alchemist in Political Strategy

Generative AI, in its simplest definition, is the subset of artificial intelligence technologies that generates new content—from words to images, sounds to simulations. It is the craftsperson of the digital realm, creating materials that feel authentic to human perception yet are born from the intricate web of algorithms. In politics, this technology has the potential to architect narratives, fashion speeches, and simulate personas, all of which are tailored to resonate with specific audiences, a tool of unprecedented power in the arsenal of political machinery.

The significance of Generative AI in politics cannot be overstated. In an age where information is both weapon and currency, the ability to generate compelling content that sways public opinion is invaluable. This technology promises to deliver targeted messages with precision, speaking to individual beliefs and biases, tapping into the cultural zeitgeist, and, at times, inflating partisan divides. As such, Generative AI has become a focal point of both potential and peril in the public square, where its capability to mold thought is both an opportunity for connection and a vector for manipulation.

Yet, the rise of Generative AI is not a sudden occurrence but rather the latest evolution in the long history of data's role in political strategy. It is a culmination of a journey that began with simple demographic tallies and has advanced to complex psychographic profiling. This progress has been marked by leaps in data storage, processing power, and algorithmic sophistication—each step a building block for the next, each innovation a layer upon which the edifice of Generative AI stands.

The Evolution of Data in Political Strategy

The chronicle of data analytics within the realm of politics is a storied one, filled with incremental advancements and paradigm-shifting breakthroughs. To understand the ascent of Generative AI, one must first comprehend the journey of data analytics in politics—a journey that mirrors the broader narrative of human progress.

In the nascent days of political strategy, data was rudimentary, consisting primarily of census figures and voting records. Campaigns were a game of numbers, of simple tallies that could predict outcomes based on past behaviors. However, as the twentieth century unfolded, a more nuanced appreciation for data emerged. The advent of more sophisticated statistical methods and the introduction of computing technology allowed for the distillation of voter databases and the genesis of targeted campaign strategies. This era witnessed the first true synergy between data and politics, where the insights drawn from voter information began to shape not only the messaging of campaigns but their very foundation.

As the digital revolution took hold, the capacity to gather and analyze data expanded exponentially. Politics entered the age of big data, where every digital footprint—a like, a share, a search—could be tracked, quantified, and leveraged. Campaigns could now segment populations into ever more precise subgroups, delivering tailored messages with an efficiency that traditional methods could never match. This was the birth of microtargeting, the ability to influence not just communities or demographics but individuals.

It was during this time that a significant pivot occurred, where AI began to transition from a commercial tool, used primarily by businesses to predict consumer behavior, to a political instrument. AI's foray into the political sphere was marked by the recognition of its predictive power and its capacity to not just understand but to anticipate voter behavior. As political entities grasped the potential of AI, they began to invest in these technologies, seeking to capitalize on their predictive capabilities to gain a competitive edge.

The Political Awakening of AI

The pivotal moments where AI transitioned from a commercial tool to a political instrument are characterized by both subtle shifts and watershed events. The early 21st century brought forth a confluence of data ubiquity, computational advancement, and an appetite for political innovation that set the stage for AI's entry into the campaign arena.

In commercial sectors, AI had already begun to demonstrate its value, optimizing supply chains, personalizing customer experiences, and predicting market trends. These applications, however, were not lost on political operatives who saw parallel opportunities in the campaign trail. The same principles that predicted consumer behavior could forecast voter tendencies. AI, with its ability to analyze vast datasets and uncover hidden patterns, was ripe for political deployment.

The true awakening of AI in politics can be traced to key campaigns that harnessed data analytics to segment voters and personalize outreach. The Obama presidential campaigns of 2008 and 2012 are often cited as turning points, showcasing how data-driven strategies could mobilize voters with unprecedented effectiveness. By leveraging AI for tasks such as voter identification, sentiment analysis, and targeted messaging, these campaigns transformed the political landscape, setting a new standard for future electoral contests.

However, it was the 2016 U.S. presidential election and the Brexit referendum that underscored the potency of AI in politics, bringing it to the forefront of public consciousness. The sophisticated use of data analytics and targeted messaging, often facilitated by AI algorithms, highlighted a new era of political strategy—one that was deeply rooted in technology. The aftermath of these events brought intense scrutiny and a barrage of questions about the ethical implications of using such tools in democratic processes.

Generative AI represents the next evolutionary leap in this technological saga. Unlike previous AI applications that focused primarily on data analysis, Generative AI takes an active role in content creation. It's not just interpreting the data—it's using the data to generate persuasive text, deep fake videos, and virtual interactions that can mimic real-life political figures with alarming accuracy. The potential of Generative AI to craft

16

narratives and shape political realities has brought us to a critical juncture where the lines between human agency and algorithmic influence are increasingly blurred.

As we close this chapter, we recognize that AI's role in politics is no longer ancillary; it is central. The technology that began as a tool for corporations has now become a cornerstone of political strategy. With Generative AI, the future of political campaigns, policy-making, and even governance is being rewritten. The implications are vast and complex, encompassing ethical, legal, and social dimensions that will be unpacked in the chapters to come. The promise and peril of AI in politics are immense, and as we stand at the threshold of this new era, we must navigate with caution, wisdom, and an unyielding commitment to the democratic principles that underpin our society.

Chapter 2

Unraveling the AI Mechanisms

As we delve into the cogs and gears of Generative AI, we find ourselves peering into a realm where technology not only interprets the world but also creates within it. This chapter aims to demystify the intricate workings of Generative AI and explore its profound implications for political discourse.

The Inner Workings of Generative AI

Generative AI is akin to a modern alchemist, transmuting data into digital gold—content that can engage, persuade, and even deceive. At its core are deep learning and neural networks, sophisticated forms of machine learning inspired by the neural structure of the human brain. These networks consist of layers of interconnected nodes or 'neurons,' each layer designed to recognize patterns and features in the data it processes.

Through a process known as training, these neural networks are fed vast amounts of data—text, images, sounds—from which they learn to generate new content that mimics the input. The more data the AI is exposed to, the more refined its output becomes. This ability to learn and create is what sets Generative

AI apart, granting it the power to produce everything from realistic images to persuasive political narratives.

In the political arena, the technology behind Generative AI is harnessed to craft messages tailored to the electorate's shifting sands, sculpting campaign materials that resonate on a deeply personal level. The implications are profound: Generative AI can potentially amplify a campaign's reach and influence, shaping public opinion on a scale previously unimaginable.

Synthetic Content Creation in Politics

The creation of synthetic political content is one of the most controversial and captivating applications of Generative AI. Deepfake technology, which can generate convincing video and audio recordings, represents a quantum leap in content fabrication. With enough training data, AI can produce videos that show public figures saying or doing things that never actually happened, challenging our perception of truth and authenticity.

The potential for deepfakes in political campaigns is both tantalizing and terrifying. On the one hand, they could revolutionize the way candidates connect with voters, allowing for personalized video messages or multilingual campaign materials generated at the touch of a button. On the other, they pose unprecedented risks to the integrity of political discourse, opening the door to misinformation and manipulation on a grand scale.

Case Study: Deep fake Technology in Political Campaigns

The exploration of deep fake technology's role in political campaigns is not a speculative journey into the future—it is an urgent inquiry into a present reality. Several instances have already highlighted the technology's disruptive potential. A notable case involved a video of a political leader appearing to deliver inflammatory remarks they never actually made, which spread rapidly across social media platforms before its artificial nature was revealed.

Such cases underscore the need for a robust dialogue on the ethics and regulation of Generative AI in politics. As deepfake technology becomes more sophisticated and accessible, the mechanisms for detecting and combating synthetic content must evolve in tandem. This arms race between creation and detection will define the political use of Generative AI in the years to come.

Deep Learning and Neural Networks: The Engines of AI Creation

To truly grasp the transformative nature of Generative AI, we must first understand the technological marvel that is deep learning. Deep learning algorithms, particularly neural networks, are at the heart of what makes Generative AI so powerful and, at the same time, so potentially disruptive.

Neural networks are modeled after the human brain's architecture, albeit in a simplified form. They consist of layers of nodes or "neurons," which process input data, learn from it, and make decisions or predictions based on that learning. Deep learning involves neural networks with multiple layers that enable the handling of vast amounts of data and the extraction of complex, hierarchical features from this data. These features are what the AI uses to generate new content that resembles the original input.

In the context of politics, deep learning can be harnessed to understand and mimic the nuances of political speech, the intricacies of policy discussions, and even the emotional undertones of campaign messaging. It's this capacity for nuanced learning and creation that makes AI not just a tool for analysis, but a potential player in the political field.

However, the power of deep learning is a double-edged sword. While it can help campaigns address voter concerns more effectively, it also raises significant ethical questions. The ability of AI to generate hyper-realistic content can blur the line between fact and fabrication, making it more challenging to discern truth in the political discourse.

From Data to Deception: The Creation of Synthetic Political Content

Generative AI excels in creating content that is increasingly indistinguishable from that created by humans. This synthetic content ranges from written articles and social media posts to images and videos, including deep fakes. The process begins with the AI analyzing a dataset – a collection of speeches, for instance – to learn patterns and styles of communication. It then uses this learned information to generate new content that echoes the learned style and substance but is entirely original.

In the political realm, synthetic content creation has the potential to alter campaign strategies fundamentally. AI-generated speeches or articles can be optimized for impact, tailored to the concerns and preferences of specific voter groups. However, the same technology can fabricate content for malicious purposes, such as deep fakes that put words into the mouths of political figures or manipulate events' depiction to mislead the public.

The use of synthetic political content raises pressing questions about authenticity and trust in the political process. As Generative AI becomes more prevalent, distinguishing between genuine and AI-generated content will become increasingly challenging, potentially eroding public trust in political figures and institutions.

Generative AI: The Future of Political Campaigns

The transition of AI from a commercial tool to a political instrument has been rapid and far-reaching. Generative AI is now poised to become a mainstay in political campaigns, offering tools for personalization and engagement at a scale previously unattainable. However, this shift is not without risks.

The adoption of Generative AI in politics must be accompanied by a rigorous examination of its impact on democratic processes. The ability to generate compelling, personalized content can engage voters and invigorate campaigns, but it also opens the door to new forms of misinformation and manipulation. As we move forward, the political use of AI must be guided by ethical considerations, regulatory frameworks, and an informed public discourse.

In closing this chapter, we stand at the precipice of a new era in political strategy, where Generative AI holds the potential to reshape campaigns, governance, and the very fabric of democratic engagement. The road ahead is fraught with challenges, but also brimming with possibilities. It is up to policymakers, technologists, and citizens to navigate this road wisely, ensuring that the power of AI is harnessed for the greater good of the political process.

Chapter 3

AI on the Campaign Trail

The use of artificial intelligence (AI) in political campaigning is no longer the stuff of science fiction; it has become a strategic imperative. This chapter will explore how AI has integrated into the fabric of political campaigning, analyze its global impact, and assess its capacity for policy making and voter engagement.

AI Tools in Modern Political Strategies

In the dynamic arena of political campaigns, the advent of Artificial Intelligence (AI) has sparked a revolution, equipping strategists with tools that possess an extraordinary finesse for understanding the electorate. Campaigns, once grounded in traditional methods of voter analysis, are now embracing AI's advanced capabilities for a multitude of strategic operations that are reshaping the political landscape.

AI's integration into political strategy is multifaceted. At its most fundamental, AI serves as a predictive powerhouse, analyzing swathes of data to forecast voter turnout with remarkable accuracy. It pinpoints swing voters who could tip the balance in close races, identifies demographic shifts that might influence election results, and sifts through the noise of big data to find signals indicative of political preferences and voting behavior. This predictive capacity allows campaign teams to allocate resources more strategically, channeling their efforts and funds into regions and demographics where they can make the most impact.

Beyond prediction, AI's capacity for personalization is pioneering a new frontier in voter communication. By sifting through the digital footprints left on social media platforms, scrutinizing public records, and interpreting patterns of consumer behavior, AI tools are crafting messages with laser-focused precision. These messages are not mere broadsides aimed at the masses; they are meticulously tailored communications that resonate on a personal level, speaking to the concerns, aspirations, and values of individual voters or finely segmented groups.

This degree of personalization heralds a leap forward in political advertising. Instead of the one-size-fits-all approach, AI enables a nuanced, micro-targeted strategy that can significantly enhance voter engagement. Political ads, policy endorsements, and campaign narratives are no longer just broadcasted; they are dialogue, initiated and informed by AI's insights into the electorate's pulse.

The ability to personalize also extends to real-time campaign management. AI doesn't just predict; it adapts. As voter sentiment shifts, AI tools adjust the campaign's messaging, ensuring that communication is always attuned to the current mood and context of the electorate. This dynamic approach keeps campaigns agile and responsive, allowing them to navigate the turbulent waters of public opinion with an informed confidence previously unattainable.

In the hands of campaign managers, AI has become a formidable ally. It is a tool that enhances human intuition with empirical insights, transforming guesswork into strategy, and strategy into success. As AI continues to evolve, its role in crafting political messages promises to become even more sophisticated, with the potential to not just influence the outcomes of elections but to redefine the very nature of political engagement.

With every election cycle, AI solidifies its role as a cornerstone of modern political strategy. The implications of this are profound, touching on the core of democratic engagement. As AI reshapes the way campaigns communicate with voters, the promise of a more engaged and informed electorate looms large, bringing with it the potential for a richer, more participatory democratic experience.

The Global Impact of AI in Politics

Artificial Intelligence (AI) in the political sphere is a global narrative, unfolding across a multitude of governance landscapes and electoral contexts. The reach of AI transcends national boundaries, weaving a complex tapestry of influence that connects developed and developing nations alike. In countries boasting advanced digital infrastructures, AI's sophisticated algorithms are sculpting voter profiles with an unprecedented depth of detail, enabling the crafting of campaign tactics that speak directly to the electorate's segmented concerns.

In regions where democracies are still blossoming, where the political terrain is rugged and the infrastructure nascent, AI emerges as a force multiplier. It steps in where traditional methods may falter, bridging distances and bypassing logistical hurdles to engage voters, catalyzing a participatory energy that might otherwise remain dormant. AI becomes the digital envoy of political parties, reaching out to constituents in remote corners, personalizing messages that resonate with local narratives, and ensuring that every voice has the opportunity to be heard and every vote the chance to be informed.

Yet, as AI's capabilities unfurl across the globe, they carry with them a suite of intricate challenges. The homogenization of political tactics is one such concern, as AI tools, designed to be universally applicable, can lead to a convergence of campaign strategies. This raises the specter of political monocultures, where diverse political ecosystems give way to standardized approaches that may not align with local customs or the nuanced fabric of individual societies.

The specter of foreign interference casts a long shadow over the promise of AI in politics. The ease with which AI can traverse national frontiers means that the tools and techniques that power political campaigns can easily be co-opted, traded, or appropriated across borders. This not only poses a threat to the sanctity of national sovereignty but also risks the integrity of domestic political discourse. The very same algorithms that can tailor a message to a voter's preferences can also be used to weave narratives of disinformation, to skew perceptions and to manipulate outcomes.

The potential for AI to be a vector of disinformation is perhaps one of the most vexing issues at the intersection of technology and governance. The capacity of AI to churn out convincing synthetic content—be it deep fakes, bots that mimic human social media users, or automated news articles—can be exploited to sow confusion and distrust. In a world where information is power, the ability to distort information is a power that can have profound consequences on the democratic fabric.

In essence, AI's global impact on politics is a dance of opportunity and caution. It offers the prospect of more engaged and informed political processes, of campaigns that can reach further and speak more directly to the hearts and minds of voters. But it also demands a vigilant approach to governance, to ensure that the tools of political engagement do not become weapons of political distortion. As nations grapple with these dual realities, the future of AI in politics will undoubtedly be a central narrative in the ongoing story of democracy in the digital age.

Predictive Analytics for Policy and Voter Engagement

The advent of Artificial Intelligence (AI) has ushered in a new epoch not only in the mechanics of campaign communication but also in the very essence of policy formation and voter engagement. The discipline of predictive analytics stands at the vanguard of this revolution, bestowing upon political operatives the foresight to gauge the electorate's pulse with an acuity that borders on prescience.

AI, through predictive analytics, is transforming the political landscape by arming policymakers with the tools to anticipate the public's response to proposed policies. Campaigns, once reactive and shaped by trial and error, can now proactively sculpt their policy platforms in alignment with the electorate's evolving preferences. This paradigm shift heralds an era where politics is no longer about the loudest message but the most resonant one, tailored to address the concerns and aspirations of the populace with precision.

This transformative approach to policy-making is predicated on the analysis of vast data sets—social media trends, economic indicators, demographic statistics—all synthesized through the crucible of AI to distill insights into voter sentiment. In this context, AI becomes the crucible that transmutes raw data into the gold of political capital—actionable intelligence that informs policies reflective of the collective will.

The narrative of AI's influence extends to the sphere of voter engagement, a realm traditionally fraught with barriers of access and apathy. AI-driven technologies, such as chatbots, are redefining the interface between campaigns and citizens, facilitating a two-way conversation that was once a logistical challenge. These AI interlocutors, capable of engaging with voters on a range of issues, from policy details to voting logistics, are democratizing the flow of information. They stand as digital sentinels, guiding voters through the labyrinth of electoral processes and empowering them with the knowledge to participate meaningfully in the democratic dialogue.

AI's foray into voter engagement also manifests in the personalization of political discourse. Chatbots, powered by natural language processing algorithms, can tailor conversations to the individual voter, addressing their unique concerns and questions with a level of personal attention previously unattainable at scale. They can facilitate voter registration, demystify the complexities of policy propositions, and even galvanize support through targeted fundraising efforts. In doing so, AI is not merely a facilitator of communication; it is an active participant in the democratic process, nurturing a more informed and engaged electorate.

The potential of AI in enhancing voter engagement and policy-making is vast, offering a glimpse into a future where the democratic process is more inclusive, informed, and responsive. It promises a political paradigm where the barriers between the governors and the governed are surmounted by the bridges of technology, and where the voice of the electorate finds a more immediate and impactful resonance in the halls of power.

As we contemplate the future of AI in politics, we stand at the threshold of a new synergy between technology and democracy. The chapters that follow will delve deeper into the promise and challenges of this synergy, exploring how AI can continue to transform the political landscape in ways that empower both policymakers and the people they serve.

As we conclude this chapter, it is clear that AI has become an integral part of political campaigning, with the power to revolutionize how candidates connect with voters and how policies are crafted. However, with great power comes great responsibility. As AI continues to evolve, so too must our understanding of its implications for democracy, ensuring that its use on the campaign trail enhances rather than undermines the electoral process.

Chapter 4

Misinformation in the AI Era

The advent of Generative AI has handed us the double-edged sword of technological advancement in the political domain. As we step into the burgeoning landscape where AI tools can generate compelling narratives and simulate human interactions, we also encounter the shadow side of this technology: the propagation of misinformation. This chapter aims to dissect the phenomenon of AI-generated misinformation, its impact on society, and the ethical questions it raises within the democratic framework.

The Rise of AI-Driven Misinformation

Generative AI, with its capacity to create content nearly indistinguishable from that produced by humans, has escalated the spread of misinformation to an unprecedented level. This technology, which encompasses text, images, and videos, can fabricate media so convincingly that it becomes difficult for even the discerning eye to spot the forgery. Once the preserve of enhancing voter engagement through personalization, these advanced algorithms now risk being commandeered for the mass production of deceptive narratives.

The potency of AI-driven misinformation lies in its chameleon-like ability to adopt the guise of credible sources. It can emulate the tone of a community leader, the earnestness of an activist, or the authority of a news anchor, casting doubt on the authenticity of digital communication. This capability extends to creating entire events, speeches, or announcements that never occurred, yet could be believed by the unsuspecting viewer or reader.

Such deepfakes and synthetic constructs have the potential to rapidly undermine the information ecosystem. The dissemination of these falsehoods via social media and other digital platforms occurs at a velocity that traditional fact-checking processes are ill-equipped to handle. The algorithms that curate our newsfeeds and recommend content to us are designed for engagement, often without discerning the veracity of the content they promote. This design flaw can be exploited by malicious actors, enabling the rapid spread of misinformation that feeds into and amplifies existing social and political divisions.

The threat extends beyond individual deception; the collective impact can sway public discourse, influence electoral outcomes, and challenge the foundations of informed democracy. The integrity of elections, the cornerstone of democratic society, is at risk when the electorate's perceptions can be so easily and convincingly manipulated. AI-generated misinformation not only has the power to alter individual opinions but also to shape the collective consciousness, potentially leading to significant real-world consequences.

As Generative AI continues to evolve, its dual capacity as a tool for good or a weapon of deception becomes increasingly stark. The same algorithms that could revolutionize democratic engagement by providing personalized information to voters also hold the capacity for unprecedented manipulation. This duality presents a formidable challenge to the information ecosystem, necessitating a proactive and multifaceted response from technologists, policymakers, and the public at large.

The rise of AI-driven misinformation prompts an urgent reassessment of how we consume and trust digital content. It is a clarion call for enhanced digital literacy, more robust fact-checking mechanisms, and a reinvigorated dialogue on the ethical use of technology in public discourse. As AI's capabilities advance, so too must our vigilance and our commitment to preserving the truth in the information that shapes our societies and our democracies.

The Societal Impact of Synthetic Media

The tidal wave of synthetic media, powered by the engines of Generative AI, has swept across the societal landscape with profound implications. In an age where AI-crafted content proliferates, discerning truth from fabrication becomes a Herculean task for citizens. This erosion of trust seeps into the bedrock of our institutions and media, challenging the very notion of objective reality. As each piece of content undergoes scrutiny for its authenticity, the collective trust—a fundamental currency in public discourse—dwindles, leaving behind a society grappling with skepticism and uncertainty.

The impact of synthetic media extends beyond a general mistrust; it actively fuels societal polarization. Content, tailor-made by AI to echo and amplify preconceived notions, serves to entrench individuals within their ideological fortresses. The resulting echo chambers, constructed with the bricks of AI-generated falsehoods, cement divisions and stoke conflicts, fragmenting the societal consensus necessary for democratic discourse. As these digital chasms widen, the cohesive fabric of communities begins to fray, and the shared reality necessary for public dialogue and compromise is threatened.

Moreover, the specter of deep fakes looms large over individual lives. These hyper-realistic forgeries, capable of putting words into the mouths of public figures or simulating actions they never took, are no longer just hypothetical threats. Their deployment can shatter personal and professional reputations, with the potential to ignite scandals, disrupt elections, and incite public unrest. The casualties of such targeted synthetic attacks often find themselves in a quagmire of legal and emotional battles, seeking to reclaim tarnished reputations from the clutches of AI-assisted defamation.

The societal fabric is further strained as the distinction between satire—a cornerstone of free expression—and malicious deception becomes increasingly indistinct. The gray area expands, challenging legal systems and ethical norms to adapt. Where once satire served as a vehicle for critique and humor, the injection of AI-generated content blurs intentions, making it harder for individuals to discern the purpose behind the media they consume. This ambiguity not only stifles the spirit of satire but also raises alarm bells for the protection of privacy and the exercise of free speech in the digital era.

Synthetic media's ripple effects touch upon the essence of human connection and trust. The relationships between individuals, communities, and their leaders are predicated on the assumption of genuine communication. As AI-generated content casts a shadow of doubt over this assumption, the foundational trust necessary for societal cooperation and progress is at risk. The challenge now lies in navigating this new terrain, where synthetic media can either serve as a tool for enlightenment and entertainment or become a weapon that undermines the social contract and corrodes the pillars of civil discourse.

Navigating the Ethical Minefield

As Generative AI weaves its complex threads into the fabric of political discourse, it casts us into an ethical labyrinth where every turn presents new challenges. The utilization of AI to craft and circulate political misinformation presents a profound moral quandary that beckons us to scrutinize the roles and responsibilities of those at the helm of this technology. The ethical dimension of AI in politics is not merely a theoretical debate but a practical imperative demanding urgent and thoughtful action.

The stewards of AI technology—developers, programmers, and platform owners—are thrust into the role of gatekeepers, charged with the task of safeguarding the digital ecosystem against the misuse of their creations. Yet, the question looms: how might they, and should they, temper the winds of innovation with the weight of ethical responsibility? As AI systems grow in sophistication, crafting ever more convincing facsimiles of reality, the onus falls upon their creators to embed ethical considerations into the very code that runs these potent algorithms.

The call for ethical frameworks and governance mechanisms in the realm of AI is not a call to stifle innovation but to channel it responsibly. Such frameworks must transcend the mere technicalities of content creation and dissemination, reaching into the societal underpinnings that lend misinformation its potency. An AI algorithm that can mimic the style of a trusted news source or public figure does not operate in a vacuum; it plays upon the trust and credibility established by these entities over time. The ethical use of AI, therefore, involves not just the technology itself but also the broader context in which it operates.

Integral to navigating this ethical minefield is a commitment to education in media literacy. As the line between real and synthetic media blurs, the ability of individuals to critically assess the content they encounter becomes paramount. Educational initiatives must thus empower citizens with the skills to discern the veracity of information, to understand the workings of AI, and to recognize the hallmarks of authenticity in an increasingly artificial world.

Simultaneously, the defense against the misuse of AI is bolstered by investments in fact-checking technologies. AI that can detect its kin—other AI-generated content—becomes a critical tool in the arsenal against misinformation. The development and deployment of such counter-AI technologies are essential in maintaining the integrity of our information landscape.

Moreover, the fight against AI-driven misinformation cannot be won in isolation. It demands a collaborative effort that spans sectors and borders. Governments, tech companies, civil society, and academia must join forces, sharing knowledge and resources to combat the spread of falsehoods. This cross-sector collaboration is crucial in developing standards, sharing best practices, and fostering an environment where ethical considerations are at the forefront of AI development and deployment.

The ethical challenges presented by Generative AI in politics are as complex as they are critical. They compel us to reexamine the relationship between technology and society, innovation and its consequences, and the shared responsibility we hold in shaping an AI-augmented world that upholds our collective values and democratic ideals. As we venture deeper into the era of AI, our moral compass must guide us through the thicket of ethical dilemmas, ensuring that our journey through the digital age is both conscientious and just.

Looking Ahead: The Fight Against Misinformation

In the vanguard against AI-driven misinformation, the landscape is ever-shifting, with the advancement of algorithms continually recalibrating the battleground. To stay ahead, a dynamic and multifaceted strategy is paramount—one that encompasses the keen edge of technological innovation as well as the foundational strength of societal resilience.

Technological solutions are the first line of defense. There is a burgeoning field dedicated to the creation of AI sophisticated enough to identify its own deceptive kin. These digital sentinels, designed to sniff out deep fakes and other AI-generated fallacies, are becoming increasingly crucial. Their task is arduous, as the forgeries they seek to uncover are often imperceptibly subtle.

Yet, their development is a testament to the ingenuity and resourcefulness of technologists committed to safeguarding the truth.

Complementing these technological advancements are societal interventions aimed at fortifying the very fabric of the public's discernment. Initiatives to bolster critical thinking and digital literacy are essential, equipping individuals with the cognitive tools to navigate the murky waters of digital content. These educational endeavors are not just about teaching the mechanics of discerning real from fake but about fostering an informed skepticism that questions, verifies, and understands the digital media landscape.

The role of public policy in this struggle is both pivotal and complex. Legislators and international organizations are tasked with the Sisyphean challenge of keeping the legal framework abreast of the relentless march of technological progress. The policies they craft must be agile, responsive, and, above all, crafted through a lens that respects the delicate balance between innovation and privacy, freedom and security. It is a delicate dance, with each step taken in legislation potentially reshaping the terrain of free speech, media, and the very essence of democratic engagement.

In this concerted effort, collaboration emerges as the keystone. The synergy between tech companies, policymakers, civil society, and the academic world forms the bedrock of an effective response to misinformation. Each sector brings a unique perspective and set of skills to the table, and it is in the confluence of these diverse streams of expertise that robust solutions can be crafted. This collaboration extends beyond national borders, recognizing the global nature of the misinformation crisis and the need for a united front to address it.

The path forward is one of proactive adaptation and collective action. As AI continues to evolve, the strategies to counter misinformation must also be iterative, learning from past challenges and anticipating future ones. This proactive stance involves not only developing new technologies and educational programs but also fostering an ongoing dialogue about the role of AI in society. It is a conversation that must be inclusive, involving voices from all corners of the public sphere, and rooted in a commitment to the principles of truth, trust, and the shared values that underpin the social contract.

The fight against misinformation is, ultimately, a fight for the integrity of our shared reality. It is a campaign not just for the veracity of information but for the very idea that, in a world brimming with AI-generated content, the truth can prevail. As we look ahead, our resolve must be firm, our vision clear, and our actions united in the face of this quintessential challenge of the digital age.

Chapter 5

Lessons from the Digital Trenches

The intricate dance between technological innovation and political maneuvering is illuminated by examining past instances where AI has left its indelible mark on the political sphere. This chapter turns a reflective eye towards historical events, extracting critical lessons from the digital trenches of political warfare where AI has been both a shield and a spear.

AI's Influence in Historical Political Events

Artificial Intelligence has not only been a protagonist in the future of political narratives but has also played a defining role in shaping historical political events. Its influence stretches across a spectrum, subtly nudging voter behaviors and precipitating dramatic shifts in the court of public opinion. By tracing AI's impact through past events, we uncover a legacy that acts as a guide to understanding its transformative power and the measures needed to harness it responsibly.

The chronicles of AI in political history reveal a gradual yet significant transition. In the initial stages, pioneering campaigners adopted AI in the form of data analytics for micro-targeting—pinpointing voters with surgical precision based on demographic and psychographic data. This quiet revolution in campaign strategy set the stage for more visible and aggressive uses of technology. Political operatives began deploying social media bots, digital entities capable of mimicking human social interactions, to amplify specific narratives and manipulate online discourse. This strategy marked a significant escalation in AI's role—from a tool enhancing the efficiency of campaigns to an active agent capable of shaping political destinies.

These early applications of AI laid the groundwork for its eventual evolution into a more sophisticated presence on the political stage. Advanced voter profiling systems emerged, boasting the ability to understand the electorate's preferences, fears, and motivations with an unprecedented depth. These systems purported to predict voter behavior with high accuracy, offering a level of insight into the electorate's psyche that was previously unattainable.

The incursion of AI into politics has not been without controversy. The use of algorithms to analyze voter data raised fundamental questions about privacy and consent. The ability of AI to influence elections became a central concern, as the line between strategic campaigning and psychological manipulation began to blur. These developments prompted a reevaluation of the ethical frameworks surrounding political data use and the need for stringent protections against the exploitation of personal information.

As we reflect on AI's historical influence in politics, it becomes evident that the technology's reach extends far beyond the tactical level of campaigns. AI has the potential to redefine the relationship between political entities and the electorate, altering the mechanisms of influence and control. Its capacity to profile and predict, while powerful, brings with it the responsibility to safeguard the principles of democratic engagement.

The examination of AI's past in the political arena serves as a lesson for the present and a caution for the future. The early adoption of AI for voter targeting and the rise of social media bots illustrate both the ingenuity of political strategists and the vulnerabilities of democratic systems. These historical instances offer invaluable insights into the complex interplay between technological innovation and political processes, highlighting the need for vigilance and ethical stewardship as AI continues to shape the political narratives of tomorrow.

The Cambridge Analytica Scandal: A Case Study

The Cambridge Analytica scandal serves as a pivotal case study in the annals of AI's intersection with politics, illuminating the profound impact and the perils inherent in the misuse of data-driven technologies. The revelation that millions of individuals' data could be harvested and weaponized to influence electoral outcomes shook the very pillars of democratic institutions and public trust.

Cambridge Analytica's strategy hinged on the advanced micro-targeting of voters, leveraging a trove of personal information gleaned without user consent. The firm's approach was a sophisticated blend of psychographics and analytics, designed to deliver custom-crafted messages with pinpoint accuracy. The underlying technology was not new, but its application revealed a startling reality: personal data, when processed through the lens of AI and machine learning, could become a tool to subtly shape and steer the democratic discourse.

This event cast a stark light on the fragility of personal privacy in the era of big data. It demonstrated how quickly and easily data could be turned into a commodity, traded and utilized in ways that the original owners could neither foresee nor control. The scandal was not just about privacy infringements; it was a sobering demonstration of how the digital footprints left behind by individuals could be assembled into a powerful engine of political influence.

As the details of the scandal unfolded, it became clear that the quest for hyper-personalized campaign strategies had crossed into ethically murky waters. The fine line between tailoring political messages to individual concerns and manipulating voter behavior through covert data exploitation had been breached. Cambridge Analytica's practices underscored the need for robust data protection mechanisms and an urgent re-examination of the ethical boundaries governing AI and data analytics in the political sphere.

The scandal also highlighted the broader implications for the integrity of the electoral process. It raised questions about the safeguards needed to protect the democratic process from being undermined by new technologies capable of distorting the political narrative. The incident prompted lawmakers, technologists, and civil society to consider how to prevent such abuses of power and how to ensure that the democratic process remains free from the undue influence of hidden digital campaigns.

The legacy of the Cambridge Analytica scandal is a cautionary tale of what can happen when the immense capabilities of AI and data analytics are harnessed without adequate oversight. It is a narrative that underscores the dual capacity of technology to empower and to disenfranchise, to illuminate and to obfuscate. As AI continues to evolve and integrate more deeply into the political domain, the lessons from this case study remain ever relevant. They serve as a guide for constructing a framework that harnesses the power of AI for the public good while guarding against the threats it poses to the very fabric of democratic life.

Cybersecurity in the Safeguarding of Electoral Integrity

In the digital age, the sanctity of electoral processes is increasingly guarded not just by the vigilance of human institutions but by the fortifications of cybersecurity. As democracies around the world navigate the complexities of digitizing votes and voter information, the role of cybersecurity in safeguarding the electoral process has never been more critical. The advent of AI has added both a shield and a potential sword to this arena, offering sophisticated means to protect against cyber threats while also representing a new frontier of vulnerability.

The digitalization of voting systems—ranging from voter registration databases to electronic voting machines—has introduced new efficiencies and accessibility into the electoral process. However, it has also opened up a Pandora's box of potential cyber threats. Instances of cyber-attacks on electoral databases have demonstrated the ease with which malicious actors can exploit vulnerabilities to attempt to sway electoral outcomes or undermine public trust in the democratic process.

The imperative for robust cybersecurity measures is undebatable. The breaches of the past serve as stark lessons, illustrating that the defense of democracy's digital frontiers is a continuous battle. Cybersecurity in the context of electoral integrity encompasses more than just safeguarding data; it is about preserving public confidence in the democratic process. As AI becomes increasingly woven into the fabric of election infrastructure, it must be wielded with caution and foresight. AI has the capability to act as a sentinel, employing advanced algorithms to monitor, detect, and neutralize cyber threats. Yet, it must be acknowledged that AI systems themselves can become targets or tools of cyber warfare, necessitating a cybersecurity approach that is as adaptive and intelligent as the AI it seeks to protect.

The dual role of AI in cybersecurity reflects the broader duality of technology—it is both a tool for advancing democratic engagement and a potential threat to it. AI-driven cybersecurity solutions can scan vast networks for anomalies that might indicate a cyber-attack, they can simulate potential attack scenarios to strengthen systems, and they can respond in real-time to ongoing threats. However, the sophistication of AI also means that when such systems are compromised, the breach can be extensive and damaging.

The safeguarding of electoral integrity in the digital realm is not solely a technological challenge but a holistic one that encompasses policy, practice, and the informed participation of the electorate. The measures taken must be comprehensive, combining state-of-the-art cybersecurity technologies with ongoing public education on the importance of cybersecurity in maintaining the health of democracies.

As nations continue to digitize their electoral processes, the lessons from cybersecurity breaches must inform the development and implementation of AI systems within political frameworks. Vigilance must be the watchword, ensuring that the guardians of electoral integrity—both human and AI—are always primed to counter the evolving threats that come with an increasingly connected world. As we harness the power of AI to protect the cornerstone of democracy, we are reminded that the technology we create must be managed with a profound sense of responsibility and a steadfast commitment to the democratic principles it is meant to serve.

Chapter 6

Social Medias: The AI Amplifiers

In the digital ecosystem, social media platforms function as both battlegrounds and amplifiers in the political arena, with AI playing an increasingly significant role in this dynamic. The power of AI to shape public discourse through social media has profound implications for democracy and civic engagement. This chapter delves into the intricate relationship between AI and social media in the context of politics, the challenges of content moderation, and the dichotomy between algorithmic curation and human judgment.

AI's Role in Social Media and Political Messaging

Artificial Intelligence has become the unseen influencer in the realm of social media, subtly dictating the flow of political discourse to the scrolling eyes of the public. Platforms that host daily interactions and exchanges of viewpoints are now underpinned by AI algorithms that sift through and analyze user data, shaping the digital landscape by personalizing the content that users encounter. These algorithms are built with the goal of maximizing user engagement, often prioritizing content that provokes a strong emotional reaction, which can lead to heightened visibility for sensationalist or divisive material.

The reach of AI in political messaging extends into the heart of campaign strategy. It has endowed political operatives with the power of micro-targeting—delivering specific messages tailored to resonate with individual voters or niche groups. This precision targeting is powered by AI's ability to dissect the digital footprints left by users, crafting messages that not only engage but also sway political opinions and voting decisions. The granularity of this targeting process has introduced a new dynamic into the digital public square, where the balance of influence and power is constantly in flux.

The role of AI in social media extends beyond content curation to the creation of political advertisements that are indistinguishable from organic content. By blending seamlessly into users' feeds, AI-generated political ads can subtly shape political sentiment without overtly appearing to do so. This blurring of lines between organic discourse and AI-curated content raises ethical questions about transparency and the role of AI in democratic processes.

The prowess of AI in political messaging is not merely a matter of algorithmic efficiency; it represents a shift in the mechanisms of influence within the public domain. As political campaigns leverage AI to target voters with increasing precision, the implications for public perception and the democratic debate are significant. The convergence of AI with social media has created a new digital polis—a space where political narratives are amplified, contested, and reshaped by the invisible hand of algorithmic decision-making.

The deployment of AI in social media as a tool for political messaging is reshaping the contours of public debate and democratic engagement. Its ability to direct the flow of information and shape political narratives has transformed it into a critical component of modern political campaigns. The result is a complex web of interaction where AI algorithms influence not only what information is presented to the public but also how it is received and internalized.

As we consider the role of AI in social media and political messaging, we must navigate the complexities of a landscape where algorithmic imperatives intersect with the need for a healthy democratic discourse. The emerging reality is one where AI-driven personalization on social media platforms has a profound impact on political communication, voter behavior, and the broader public conversation. Understanding and addressing the implications of AI's role in this space is essential for ensuring that the digital arena remains a fair and equitable forum for political engagement.

The Challenge of Content Moderation

The digital landscape is awash with a constant stream of user-generated content, and within this deluge lies the formidable challenge of content moderation. Social media companies, stewards of this vast online ecosystem, are increasingly reliant on Artificial Intelligence (AI) to police the platforms, sifting through content to uphold community standards and curb the spread of misinformation. AI systems, armed with algorithms designed to detect policy violations, serve as the first line of defense against the tide of harmful content.

However, the labyrinth of human language, with its nuances, idioms, and cultural specificities, presents a formidable challenge to these digital gatekeepers. AI, for all its computational prowess, often struggles to discern the intent behind words and images. The subtleties that define satire or parody, which are readily apparent to the human eye, can elude even the most sophisticated AI, leading to instances of unjustified censorship. Similarly, regional dialects, local colloquialisms, and contextual nuances can escape AI detection, allowing potentially harmful content to slip through the cracks.

Moreover, the challenge is magnified by the sheer volume of content that cascades through social media platforms every minute. Billions of posts, tweets, images, and videos are shared, requiring a scale of moderation that is beyond the scope of human capability alone. AI steps into this breach, offering the ability to process and analyze large datasets at speeds unattainable by human moderators. Yet, this reliance on AI comes with its own set of complications. Without the tempering influence of human judgment, AI can inadvertently stifle legitimate discourse, mistaking heated political debate for hate speech, or flagging passionate advocacy as extremism.

The interplay between AI and human moderators is a delicate balancing act, where too much reliance on one can undermine the effectiveness of the other. The dance of algorithmic precision and human understanding is intricate, and when out of sync, can lead to both the over-censorship of benign content and the under-censorship of the harmful. This balancing act is further complicated by the evolving nature of language and political discourse. As societal norms shift and new forms of expression emerge, AI systems must continuously learn and adapt, a process that requires a nuanced understanding of the ever-changing social and cultural landscape.

In the arena of content moderation, AI has the potential to act as a powerful ally in the fight against misinformation and the maintenance of civil discourse. Yet, the challenges it faces in distinguishing the permissible from the prohibited, the contentious from the offensive, are steep. The implications of these challenges are not trivial; they touch upon the core values of free expression and the right to information. As social media companies and technologists navigate this terrain, the sophistication of AI in understanding the complex tapestry of human communication must evolve. It is a pursuit that is critical not only to the integrity of social media platforms but also to the preservation of the vibrant, dynamic exchange of ideas that is essential to the health of democratic societies.

Algorithmic Curation versus Human Judgment

The digital sphere is dominated by an intricate interplay between algorithmic curation and human judgment, a duality that sits at the crux of modern social media and its intersection with politics. Algorithms boast the ability to parse through data at an unprecedented scale, but they operate devoid of the innate human sensibilities that comprehend the complex tapestry of social and political life. Their logic is binary, while human judgment thrives on spectrums and subtleties. This dichotomy underscores a profound debate on the governance of digital spaces where political ideas are shared and shaped.

Algorithms, the bedrock of AI, are tasked with curating content for billions of users, yet they are fundamentally programmed by human hands, guided by human-devised objectives, and imbued with human-crafted biases. The parameters within which they operate are set with the intention to engage, but without the nuanced understanding of cultural and contextual variances that give meaning to human communication. As a result, the content that these algorithms elevate or suppress can reflect underlying predispositions, leading to concerns about the fairness and impartiality of AI moderation systems.

Transparency in the mechanisms of AI decision-making is pivotal, yet it often remains shrouded in layers of complexity, inaccessible to the average user and, at times, to the creators themselves. This opacity raises pressing questions about accountability in the digital realm—about who, or what, is responsible when AI systems inadvertently silence a political dissident or amplify a harmful conspiracy theory.

Striking the right balance between the efficiency of AI and the discernment of human oversight is not just a technical challenge; it's a fundamental aspect of digital stewardship. It is about shaping a virtual public square that respects human dignity, values democratic dialogue, and reflects the diverse mosaic of human thought. The calibration of this balance is crucial; too much reliance on AI, and we risk creating an echo chamber shaped by invisible hands, too little, and the deluge of content becomes unmanageable, with potential misinformation slipping through the digital cracks.

The quest for equilibrium demands a symbiotic relationship between AI and human moderators, one where algorithms are designed not just for optimality of performance but also for the optimality of democratic engagement. Human moderators serve as the arbiters of context, the interpreters of nuance, and the safeguard against the overreach of AI. Their role is to ensure that the content promoted by algorithms aligns with the values of the platform and the expectations of its users.

As social media continues to evolve as a central arena for political discourse, the interplay of algorithmic curation and human judgment must also progress. It must become more sophisticated, more transparent, and more aligned with the principles of democratic society. The task at hand is not to eschew the power of AI but to harness it, to create digital environments that are reflective of human diversity and conducive to the robust exchange of ideas. In navigating the delicate balance between AI's scalability and human sensibility, the aim is to craft digital spaces that facilitate the flow of information while upholding the integrity of political conversation and debate.

As we delve deeper into the relationship between AI and social media within the political landscape, it becomes clear that the technology that connects us also has the power to divide. The decisions made by AI algorithms can have far-reaching consequences for democratic engagement, making the governance of these algorithms and the design of social media platforms matters of public interest. The future of political discourse in the digital age depends on our ability to navigate the complexities of this relationship, ensuring that social media remains a tool for democratic expression rather than a weapon against it.

Chapter 7

The Legal and Ethical Conundrum

As Artificial Intelligence (AI) becomes a staple in the digital dissemination of political messaging, a labyrinth of legal and ethical considerations comes to the fore. This chapter endeavors to untangle the intricate web of laws and moral principles surrounding the use of AI in the political sphere, charting the waters where technological capabilities intersect with the need for ethical governance.

Regulatory Challenges in the Age of AI

The integration of Artificial Intelligence (AI) into the political fabric has ushered in an era of regulatory challenges that traditional legal frameworks are struggling to contend with. As the velocity of AI innovation outpaces the legislative process, existing regulations around political advertising, data privacy, and the mechanisms of campaigning are pushed to their breaking point. AI's capacity to dissect and utilize vast datasets for voter targeting and message optimization is prompting a reexamination of the principles that govern political engagement and the safeguarding of democratic integrity.

One of the most pressing concerns is the transparency of AI operations within the political sphere. The algorithms that drive political messaging and voter targeting operate within black boxes, often impenetrable to outside scrutiny, raising questions about the visibility of AI's role in shaping political narratives. The accountability of AI-driven campaigns, particularly when they err or cross ethical lines, becomes difficult to ascertain, clouding the waters of political responsibility.

In the context of electioneering, AI's capabilities to influence public opinion through automated processes present lawmakers with the challenge of redefining the scope and limits of political influence. The micro-targeting capabilities of AI, powered by deep learning and complex data analytics, are transforming the ways voters are approached and engaged. This granular level of targeting is not something current election laws were designed to address, leaving a gap in the regulatory fabric that needs to be stitched with new legal threads.

Data privacy stands at the center of the regulatory conundrum posed by AI in politics. As political campaigns increasingly rely on AI to process personal information for strategic advantage, the boundaries of data usage and individual privacy rights come into question. Laws that were crafted in a pre-AI era are now being tested by the capabilities of machine learning algorithms to parse through personal data and extract actionable insights for political advantage.

Legislators are thus confronted with the formidable task of drafting new laws or amending existing ones to capture the multifaceted realities introduced by AI. This legislative overhaul requires not just a technical understanding of AI's capabilities but a deep engagement with the democratic values at stake. Laws must be designed to ensure that AI is harnessed for political activities in a manner that is fair, transparent, and accountable, reflecting the democratic ideals that form the bedrock of society.

Moreover, the lawmaking process itself must adapt to the pace of technological change. It calls for agile legislative mechanisms that can respond swiftly to the evolution of AI technologies, ensuring that regulations remain relevant and effective. The development of such adaptive legal frameworks is critical to maintaining the integrity of electoral processes and protecting the democratic process from being compromised by unchecked AI interventions.

Navigating the regulatory challenges in the age of AI requires a concerted effort that brings together legislators, technologists, legal experts, and civil society. It is a collaborative journey toward crafting a legal environment that can accommodate the complexities of AI while upholding the principles of democracy. As AI continues to reshape the political landscape, the imperative for robust and forward-looking regulations becomes increasingly clear, demanding attention, action, and innovation from all corners of the political and legal spectrum.

The Ethics of AI-Driven Political Influence

In the realm of political strategy, the deployment of Artificial Intelligence (AI) has opened up ethical frontiers that mirror the complexities of the technology itself. The influence AI wields over public opinion and the electoral process is profound, necessitating a vigilant ethical appraisal. The central question is no longer confined to AI's capability but extends to its moral application within the political sphere.

The ethical challenges of AI in politics are manifold. At its core, AI holds the power to craft messages with a precision that, while maximizing impact, also raises the specter of manipulation. When political campaigns use AI to distill vast amounts of personal data into targeted communication, they walk a fine line between persuasion and influence that veers towards coercion. The distinction between informed influence and subtle indoctrination becomes increasingly blurred as AI-driven messages are tailored to align closely with individual biases and beliefs.

The power to shape political narratives through AI comes with the imperative to honor the principles of truth and fairness. The burgeoning use of AI tools to analyze behavior and predict political leanings must be tempered with a commitment to ethical standards that protect individual autonomy and prevent the erosion of democratic engagement. Political entities that leverage AI must do so with a heightened sense of responsibility, ensuring that the technology serves to inform and engage rather than to deceive and divide.

Ethical considerations surrounding AI extend to the heart of personal data usage. The moral implications of mining personal information for political gain are significant, raising questions about the right to privacy and the sanctity of the individual's digital identity. AI's ability to segment and target individuals based on their digital footprints challenges the notion of informed consent and the autonomy of the electorate.

Furthermore, the creation of hyper-personalized political content by AI systems invites a critical evaluation of the boundaries of ethical political communication. As AI algorithms generate content that resonates on a deeply personal level, the potential for influencing electoral outcomes in ways that may not be transparent or fair becomes a pressing ethical issue. The prospect of AI tools shaping electoral narratives to the extent that they could sway election results underscores the need for a robust ethical framework that governs the use of such technology.

The intersection of AI and ethics in politics is not just about the potential for abuse but also about the opportunity to enhance democratic processes. Ethical AI use can foster a more informed and engaged electorate, but achieving this ideal requires a conscientious approach to technology deployment, one that upholds the values of democratic societies.

As political campaigns increasingly integrate AI into their strategies, the ethical ramifications of this technology must be carefully considered. This involves a collective effort to define and enforce ethical guidelines that govern AI's role in politics. Such guidelines should ensure that AI's power to influence is wielded with integrity, enhancing the democratic process rather than undermining it. Maintaining the electorate's trust and the legitimacy of democratic institutions depends on the ethical stewardship of AI, a challenge that demands attention and action from all stakeholders in the political ecosystem.

International Perspectives on AI Regulation

The encroachment of Artificial Intelligence (AI) into the political sphere is a global phenomenon that transcends borders and political systems. Nations around the world confront a myriad of challenges and opportunities that AI presents, navigating through uncharted regulatory waters. The response to AI's rise in politics has been varied, with countries crafting a mosaic of regulatory responses that mirror their unique cultural, legal, and political landscapes.

This international regulatory patchwork is characterized by diverse approaches to the governance of AI, reflecting differing national priorities and values, particularly regarding privacy, freedom of expression, and the fundamental mechanics of political rights. Some countries have forged ahead, creating comprehensive AI governance frameworks that aim to address the multifaceted implications of AI in politics, from campaign practices to voter privacy. These pioneering frameworks often attempt to strike a balance between fostering technological innovation and protecting democratic integrity.

Conversely, other nations find themselves at the preliminary stages, still contemplating the foundational principles that should underpin AI regulation in the political realm. The disparity in regulatory approaches is indicative of the broader conversation about the role of AI in society and the varying levels of preparedness and perspectives that different governments bring to the table.

The need for international cooperation and dialogue in this context is paramount. As AI technologies do not adhere to national boundaries, their political applications have implications that ripple across the globe. The sharing of regulatory experiences, successes, and pitfalls is invaluable as it allows countries to learn from one another and to craft regulations that are informed by a wider array of insights and expertise.

This international discourse is not merely academic; it has practical significance in fostering a set of shared best practices for AI governance in politics. Such collaborative efforts can lead to the creation of guidelines that not only serve the interests of individual nations but also address the collective challenges that democracies face in the age of AI. By harmonizing regulatory efforts, countries can ensure that AI is used in ways that enhance political processes and safeguard democratic values, rather than undermining them.

The global dialogue on AI regulation in politics also provides an opportunity to establish international norms and agreements that can guide the ethical deployment of AI by political actors. These norms could potentially cover a broad spectrum of AI's political uses, from election advertising and voter engagement to the dissemination of political news and the security of electoral infrastructure.

As countries navigate the complexities of AI regulation in politics, they are laying the groundwork for the future governance of a technology that is rapidly becoming integral to the political fabric of societies worldwide. The collective endeavor to regulate AI in politics is not just a response to a technological trend but a proactive measure to shape the trajectory of democracies in the digital age. It is a pursuit that requires not only legal and technical acumen but also a commitment to the democratic principles that AI, if properly harnessed, has the potential to strengthen.

Navigating the legal and ethical conundrum of AI in politics is a complex endeavor that requires the collective efforts of legislators, technologists, ethicists, and the public. It is a journey that must be undertaken with care and deliberation, as the decisions made today will shape the role of AI in the political landscapes of tomorrow. As societies continue to evolve alongside advancing technologies, the dialogue surrounding AI's place in politics must remain open, informed, and focused on preserving the integrity and vitality of democratic governance.

Chapter 8

Safeguarding Democracy

In the digital era, where the landscape of political engagement is continually reshaped by technological advancements, defending democracy against the risks posed by Artificial Intelligence (AI) becomes a paramount concern. This chapter addresses the multifaceted strategies needed to mitigate the threats AI poses to the electoral process, focusing on the development of detection technologies, the importance of voter education, and the collaborative efforts required to uphold democratic integrity.

Detection Technologies for AI-Generated Content

In the escalating battle between the creation and detection of AI-generated content, the development of sophisticated detection technologies is critical. As artificial intelligence becomes more skilled at crafting content that is indistinguishable from that created by humans, the tools needed to uncover these digital illusions must advance in tandem. Researchers and technologists are on the front lines, engineering advanced systems capable of identifying deepfakes, distinguishing AI-authored text, and pinpointing the digital footprints of fabricated media.

These detection systems are often powered by AI algorithms designed to discern subtle inconsistencies or hallmarks of artificiality that may go unnoticed by the human eye. Machine learning models are trained on vast datasets of both genuine and synthetic content, learning to recognize the ever-so-slight deviations from authenticity that mark the work of their AI counterparts. As AI technology refines its ability to simulate reality, these detection models must similarly evolve, becoming more nuanced and responsive to emerging techniques in content manipulation.

The rapid advancement of AI content generators means that the algorithms designed to detect them cannot remain static. They must be dynamic and adaptable, learning from each encounter with new forms of synthetic media. This technological arms race is not merely a challenge of engineering but a matter of safeguarding public discourse. The integrity of information channels—upon which democracies rely for an informed electorate—depends significantly on the ability to separate fact from cleverly constructed fiction.

The imperative to develop robust detection technologies for AI-generated content is thus twofold. Technologically, it requires continuous innovation and refinement of tools that can keep pace with the advancing capabilities of content generators. From a societal perspective, it demands a commitment to maintaining the channels of information that are foundational to the electoral process and democratic debate. The success of these technologies in identifying and flagging inauthentic content will play a crucial role in preserving the trustworthiness of media and the veracity of the digital ecosystem.

In the quest to maintain the authenticity of the information that flows through our digital lives, the development of detection technologies is a pivotal endeavor. It bridges the gap between the rapid growth of AI's ability to generate realistic content and the necessity for the public to rely on the information they receive. As society grows increasingly reliant on digital media for news, communication, and political discourse, ensuring the reliability of this media becomes a public imperative.

The stakes in developing AI-powered detection technologies are high, as the veracity of digital content underpins not only individual decision-making but also the collective choices of societies. The task of ensuring that these technologies are robust, accessible, and continually advancing is critical in the fight against misinformation. It is a challenge that calls for the brightest minds in technology, the most forward-thinking policies in governance, and an unwavering commitment to the public good in the age of digital democracy.

Voter Education and Media Literacy Initiatives

In an era increasingly dominated by Artificial Intelligence (AI), the safeguarding of democratic processes necessitates not only the advancement of detection technologies but also the fortification of the electorate through education. Media literacy initiatives have emerged as essential instruments in this defense, empowering voters to critically navigate the burgeoning complexity of the information landscape. Such initiatives are instrumental in cultivating an electorate adept at discerning the veracity of sources, distinguishing between credible information and potential misinformation, and comprehending the underlying mechanisms of AI-generated content.

The cornerstone of media literacy in the context of AI is the enhancement of the public's evaluative skills. As the lines between human-created and machine-generated content blur, the ability to assess the credibility of information becomes a vital competency for every digital citizen. Media literacy programs strive to instill these critical thinking skills, enabling voters to scrutinize the intent, origin, and authenticity of the political content they encounter online. This educational push aims to build a populace that is not only informed but also resilient against the waves of deceptive content that AI can propagate.

Simultaneously, voter education programs are expanding their focus to include a deeper understanding of AI's role within political campaigning. These educational initiatives shed light on the intricacies of data-driven campaign strategies, elucidating how personal data can be leveraged to micro-target voters with alarming precision. They unravel the complex tapestry of

71

algorithmic curation, revealing how these unseen mechanisms can influence the flow of political discourse and potentially introduce bias into the information ecosystem.

The dialogue around voter education also encompasses the critical issues of data privacy and the ethical use of personal information in the digital age. As voters become more aware of how their data may be utilized by political entities, they grow increasingly vigilant, fostering a culture of privacy awareness and informed consent. An electorate cognizant of their digital rights is a formidable force, one that is less prone to manipulation and more inclined to hold political actors and platforms to account.

The push for voter education and media literacy is not merely a response to the challenges posed by AI but a proactive measure to strengthen the very foundations of democracy. By ensuring that voters are educated about the digital tools and tactics employed in political campaigns, society can cultivate a more transparent and equitable political environment. This environment encourages informed participation, critical engagement, and a healthy skepticism that serves as a bulwark against the potential abuses of AI in politics.

As AI continues to reshape the landscape of political communication and campaigning, the imperative for comprehensive voter education and media literacy programs becomes increasingly clear. It is through these initiatives that voters can be equipped with the knowledge and tools necessary to navigate the digital age's complexities, fostering a democracy that is robust, vibrant, and reflective of an informed and engaged electorate. These educational endeavors stand as a testament to the enduring power of an informed populace in the face of technological change and as a beacon of defense in the ongoing effort to preserve the integrity of democratic institutions.

Policy and Industry Efforts to Safeguard Elections

The integrity of electoral processes in the face of burgeoning AI technologies calls for a concerted defense, marshaling the collective forces of policy and industry. This critical task demands that governments and tech companies not only coalesce around shared objectives but also drive forward with initiatives tailored to the nuances of digital-age politics. Safeguarding democracy from AI's potential perils is a multifaceted mission that spans legislation, technological innovation, and the enforcement of ethical standards.

Governments are tasked with the formidable challenge of crafting policies that navigate the complex interplay between technological advancement and electoral integrity. This legislative endeavor involves the creation of regulations that ensure AI is utilized ethically within the electoral context, particularly in relation to the handling of personal data.

Policymakers must also focus on fortifying the security of election infrastructure, making it impervious to AI-related threats that range from disinformation campaigns to cyber-attacks on voting systems. These policies must be agile, evolving in step with the rapid advancements in AI to remain effective in their protective role.

Parallel to the legislative push, the tech industry bears a significant share of responsibility in safeguarding elections. Companies at the helm of AI development and deployment are called upon to establish and uphold rigorous standards that curtail the misuse of AI on their platforms. This includes the crafting and enforcement of robust content moderation policies that can identify and mitigate the spread of misleading information. Furthermore, the industry must strive for transparency in algorithmic operations, ensuring that the underlying processes of AI tools are understandable and accountable to the public they serve.

The tech industry's role extends to the development of AI systems that bolster rather than weaken democratic practices. These systems should enhance the accessibility and reliability of information, enabling voters to make informed decisions free from covert AI influence. It is incumbent upon tech companies to demonstrate a commitment to democracy that is as steadfast as their pursuit of innovation.

Beyond the realms of policy and industry, the broader ecosystem of civil society, academia, and international bodies plays a critical role in the defense of democratic elections. These entities act as watchdogs, thought leaders, and standard-bearers, advocating for ethical practices and contributing to the dialogue on AI governance. Their oversight is crucial in holding both governments and tech companies accountable, ensuring that the stewardship of AI in politics is conducted with the public interest at heart.

Additionally, the academic community contributes to safeguarding elections by advancing research into AI's impact on democracy and by developing new technologies that enhance electoral security and transparency. International organizations facilitate cross-border collaboration, fostering the exchange of best practices and supporting the development of global norms that can guide the responsible use of AI in the political domain.

The collective endeavor to safeguard elections in the AI era is a testament to the shared commitment to democratic values. It is through the synthesis of policy rigor, industry integrity, and community vigilance that elections can be shielded from the risks AI poses. This collaborative approach not only fortifies electoral processes against immediate threats but also lays the groundwork for a future in which AI serves to strengthen rather than subvert the democratic fabric of societies worldwide.

As we venture into the depths of what it means to defend democracy in an age where AI's influence is ever-growing, a comprehensive approach is required—one that combines technology, education, and policy. It is a multi-layered defense system, with each component reinforcing the other, to ensure that the democratic values we cherish are upheld in the face of AI's transformative power. The strategies outlined in this chapter are not exhaustive, but they provide a foundation upon which a robust defense of democracy can be built, ensuring that the electoral process remains fair, transparent, and resilient in the face of AI's challenges.

Chapter 9

AI for Good - Enhancing Participation and Fair Play

In a landscape often shadowed by concerns over AI's misuse, there is a brighter narrative to be told. Artificial Intelligence (AI) possesses an equally powerful potential to enhance democratic processes and foster fair play in the electoral system. This chapter explores the constructive applications of AI that support the pillars of democracy: participation, transparency, and equity.

AI's Role in Voter Access and Engagement

Artificial Intelligence (AI) is increasingly being recognized as a powerful tool to democratize political participation, facilitating broader engagement across the electorate. By leveraging AI, new platforms are emerging that offer voters streamlined access to information about political candidates and issues, presented in a way that resonates with their personal interests and understanding. This personalized approach to voter education can lead to a more informed electorate, better equipped to make decisions at the polls.

The potential of AI to make the electoral process more accessible is vast. For instance, AI applications are simplifying the voter registration process, providing timely reminders to encourage electoral participation, and offering clear, concise information on the logistics of voting. Such AI-driven initiatives aim to remove the friction from participating in elections, addressing common barriers that can deter people from exercising their democratic rights.

In the pursuit of inclusivity, AI's ability to transcend language and accessibility barriers presents a significant opportunity. Natural language processing and machine translation are being employed to ensure that election-related materials are available in a multitude of languages, reflecting the linguistic diversity of the population. By providing multilingual resources, AI helps to ensure that language is not an impediment to political participation.

Moreover, AI's adaptability is being leveraged to assist voters with disabilities, an often-overlooked demographic in the political sphere. AI-powered tools, including voice-activated systems and customized content delivery, cater to a range of needs, making political content more accessible than ever before. Such innovations reflect a commitment to equality in the democratic process, ensuring every individual has the opportunity to be an active participant in their governance.

AI's role in voter access and engagement is not limited to the period leading up to elections. It also encompasses the development of platforms that facilitate ongoing interaction between citizens and their representatives. Through AI-enhanced communication channels, voters can express their views, seek clarification on policies, and remain engaged with the political process beyond the ballot box.

By harnessing the capabilities of AI, the barriers that have traditionally hindered electoral participation can be dismantled. The technology's ability to provide tailored information, overcome language obstacles, and cater to diverse needs positions AI as a critical ally in the effort to ensure that every voice is heard. In the hands of those committed to democratic ideals, AI can help create a political landscape that is more accessible, more inclusive, and more attuned to the needs and rights of the electorate.

As we explore the role of AI in enhancing voter access and engagement, it becomes apparent that the technology holds the key to unlocking a more dynamic and participatory form of democracy. The implications of this are profound, as a more engaged electorate is foundational to the health and vitality of democratic societies. AI, therefore, stands not just as a technological tool but as a transformative force with the potential to redefine the very experience of democratic participation.

Successful Implementations of AI in Electoral Contexts

The potential of Artificial Intelligence (AI) to positively transform electoral systems has been demonstrated in various successful implementations worldwide. These examples not only showcase AI's capacity to enhance the efficiency of the voting process but also its role in safeguarding the integrity of elections and contributing to more informed policy-making.

Innovative AI systems have been adopted in certain jurisdictions to streamline the logistical challenges of voting. By integrating AI technologies, electoral authorities have effectively reduced queues and wait times at polling stations, a perennial issue that has discouraged voter turnout in the past. These AI solutions facilitate a smoother voting experience, offering real-time assistance to those in need of guidance, and ensuring that the physical act of casting a ballot is as convenient as possible for every voter.

Moreover, AI has taken on the role of a vigilant guardian in the sphere of election integrity. Sophisticated pattern recognition algorithms are now capable of monitoring voting patterns and flagging irregularities that may suggest fraudulent activities or procedural malpractices. This application of AI acts as a powerful deterrent against attempts to undermine the electoral process and bolsters public confidence in the fairness and accuracy of election results.

Beyond the mechanics of the election day, AI's influence extends to understanding the electorate itself. Predictive analytics, a field in which AI excels, is being leveraged to gain deeper insights into voter needs and preferences. This data-driven approach enables governments to engage in more responsive governance, tailoring policies and initiatives to better meet the expectations and requirements of their constituents.

AI's capacity for predictive modeling has also found its way into the legislative arena. AI tools are increasingly being utilized to project the outcomes of policy decisions, simulating the effects of proposed legislation on various demographic and socio-economic groups within the population. This allows policymakers to anticipate the repercussions of their initiatives, helping to avoid unintended consequences and ensuring that policy decisions are grounded in empirical evidence rather than conjecture.

These successful deployments of AI in electoral contexts reflect the technology's versatility and its potential to serve the public good. By optimizing the voting process, enhancing the integrity of elections, and aiding in the formulation of responsive policies, AI has demonstrated its value as a tool for democratic enhancement.

As these instances of AI's application in elections become more widespread, they offer valuable lessons and frameworks that can be adapted and implemented in other regions. The experiences gained from these pioneering uses of AI in electoral systems provide a blueprint for harnessing the technology to serve democratic ends—making the process of voting more accessible, ensuring the reliability of election outcomes, and contributing to the creation of well-informed, data-driven public policies.

The advancements of AI in electoral contexts serve as a harbinger of the technology's transformative potential for democratic practices. While these applications are just the beginning, they pave the way for a future where AI not only supports but strengthens the foundations of democracy, fostering an environment where the electoral process is not only secure and efficient but also more aligned with the will and welfare of the people.

Future Prospects for AI in Democratic Enhancement

As we cast our gaze into the future, Artificial Intelligence (AI) looms large as a transformative force in the realm of democracy. The potential applications of AI promise to redefine the democratic experience, making it more inclusive, secure, and aligned with the electorate's collective voice. AI's evolution carries the promise of reshaping election methodologies, offering solutions that could enhance the accessibility and integrity of voting while safeguarding the sanctity of every individual's ballot.

One of the most significant prospects for AI lies in the domain of voter verification. With the development of more advanced AI systems, the process of identifying voters could become more robust, curbing the risk of electoral fraud. AI could offer sophisticated biometric solutions that ensure the person casting the vote is who they claim to be, all while upholding stringent standards of privacy and data security. Such technologies could strike a delicate balance between preventing illicit voting practices and protecting voters' personal information from misuse.

Beyond the mechanics of voting, AI holds the potential to catalyze more participatory democratic models. AI-powered platforms are already beginning to emerge, platforms capable of synthesizing public opinions and feedback on a massive scale. These systems can aggregate the collective viewpoints of a diverse population, analyze sentiment on policy issues, and present this data in a manner that is digestible for both citizens and policymakers. The implication is a shift toward a more dialogic form of democracy, where the gap between public sentiment and policy-making is significantly narrowed.

AI's capabilities could also enhance the deliberative aspects of democracy. By facilitating the organization and analysis of public forums, debates, and consultations, AI can help distill the vast array of ideas and arguments into actionable insights. This could lead to policy development that is more reflective of the public's consensus, offering a counterbalance to the traditional top-down approach to governance.

Moreover, AI has the potential to empower citizens to play a more active role in the legislative process. By utilizing AI to model the potential impacts of policy decisions, citizens can gain a clearer understanding of how such policies might affect their lives. This level of understanding can lead to more informed public discourse and higher levels of engagement in the political process.

The landscape that AI could help create is one where the distance between the electorate and their representatives is significantly reduced. AI-driven tools could support continuous interaction and engagement, fostering a democratic environment that is not only reactive during election cycles but also proactive in everyday governance.

As we contemplate the future of AI in the enhancement of democracy, the possibilities are as profound as they are promising. AI has the potential to be a cornerstone in building more dynamic, transparent, and participatory political systems, where the principles of democracy are not only upheld but invigorated. The journey towards this future will require careful navigation, ensuring that the deployment of AI in the democratic sphere is guided by ethical considerations and a commitment to the public good. With thoughtful implementation, AI could be pivotal in crafting a democratic future that is robust, resilient, and resonant with the aspirations of the global citizenry.

Chapter 10

The Road Ahead for AI and Elections

The intersection of Artificial Intelligence (AI) and electoral politics is poised to redefine the relationship between citizens and their governments. As we look toward the future, it is clear that AI has the potential to alter the political landscape in profound and enduring ways. This chapter explores the anticipatory steps that must be taken to prepare for a new political reality shaped by AI, the evolution of AI's role in political strategy, and the strategies for balancing innovation with the preservation of democratic values.

Anticipated Technological Advancements in AI and Politics

The horizon of political campaigning and electoral management is being redrawn by the continuous advancements in Artificial Intelligence (AI). The promise of AI to transform politics into a more data-centric and personalized affair is unfolding rapidly. As AI becomes increasingly sophisticated, it is anticipated to empower political campaigns with tools that can tailor messages to individual voters with remarkable precision, thereby enhancing the impact and reach of political narratives.

These tools are expected to harness the vast amounts of data generated by voters' online and offline activities, employing advanced algorithms to predict voter behavior with greater accuracy. This capability could revolutionize campaign strategies, enabling political actors to deploy resources more efficiently and connect with voters in more meaningful ways. The granular level of targeting possible with AI may not only refine voter mobilization efforts but also allow for the presentation of policies in a manner that resonates with individual concerns and values.

Furthermore, AI is poised to play a pivotal role in the evolution of electoral integrity and trust. The integration of blockchain technology in digital voting systems promises to create an immutable ledger of votes, offering a robust defense against tampering and fraud. When coupled with AI, blockchain could ensure real-time verification and authentication of electoral processes, from voter registration to the final tally of votes.

Additionally, biometric technologies, such as facial recognition, are being explored as methods to enhance the security of the voting process. AI-powered biometric verification can provide a secure means of ensuring that the person casting the vote is eligible to do so, potentially reducing the scope of electoral fraud. These technologies, by safeguarding the authenticity of each vote, can contribute significantly to the legitimacy of elections.

The integration of AI in the electoral arena is also anticipated to foster greater transparency. AI systems could enable a more open view of the electoral process, allowing voters to track their ballots and gain insights into the vote-counting process. This transparency is crucial in building public confidence in the electoral system, encouraging broader participation and fostering a stronger democratic culture.

As we look to the future, the interplay between AI and electoral politics is set to deepen, driven by a mutual reinforcement of technological innovation and democratic values. The tools and systems under development have the potential to enhance the responsiveness of political campaigns, the security of voting mechanisms, and the overall trust in the electoral system.

These anticipated advancements in AI bring with them a wealth of opportunities to bolster the democratic process. By making elections more accessible, secure, and reflective of the electorate's preferences, AI stands to not only transform the mechanics of how we vote but also to enrich the democratic experience itself. The trajectory of AI in politics points toward a future where the electorate is more engaged, where campaigns are more responsive, and where the sanctity of each vote is diligently preserved.

The Changing Face of Political Strategy in the Age of AI

The advent of Artificial Intelligence (AI) is ushering in a transformative era for political strategy, marking a departure from traditional approaches and towards a data-driven, algorithmically-informed landscape. In this new age, political campaigns are poised to become highly dynamic entities, with AI providing the strategic compass to navigate the ever-evolving preferences and sentiments of the public.

AI's analytical capabilities are transforming the way political strategies are conceived and implemented. By leveraging real-time data analysis, campaigns can pivot and adapt strategies with a level of responsiveness that was previously unattainable. The utilization of AI for predictive modeling and scenario simulations offers a foresight into the potential efficacy of different campaign approaches, equipping political actors with the insights needed to optimize their outreach and messaging for maximum impact.

The influence of AI in political campaigning is not just a matter of operational logistics; it extends to the heart of policy formation and public issue engagement. AI's ability to sift through the vast digital conversations happening across social media platforms and other public forums enables a more nuanced understanding of the electorate's pulse. By identifying patterns in public feedback and discourse, AI tools can surface emerging concerns and priorities, providing politicians with a data-rich perspective on the issues that resonate most strongly with their constituents.

These insights, derived from AI's deep analysis, have the potential to inform policy development in a manner that is both timely and aligned with public sentiment. As AI models become more sophisticated, they can offer predictive insights into the likely public reception of proposed policies or legislative changes, allowing for a proactive approach to governance that anticipates and meets the needs of the populace.

The integration of AI into political strategy also raises the potential for more personalized and targeted policy communication. AI's data processing capabilities enable the segmentation of the electorate into distinct groups based on shared concerns or preferences, allowing for tailored policy messaging that speaks directly to the specific interests of different voter blocs. This degree of personalization, while powerful, also necessitates careful consideration to ensure it supports informed democratic choice rather than manipulative targeting.

As political strategies evolve in tandem with AI's advancements, the implications for democratic engagement are profound. AI has the capacity to make political campaigns more informed by the electorate's concerns, more adaptable to changing public opinion, and more strategic in their deployment of resources. However, this evolution also calls for a rigorous examination of the ethical dimensions of AI in political strategy, ensuring that these powerful tools are used in ways that enhance democratic processes rather than undermine them.

In summary, AI is set to redefine the fabric of political strategy, offering new tools for analysis, engagement, and policy-making. As we step into this new paradigm, the challenge for political actors and technologists alike will be to navigate the AI revolution with a commitment to the values of transparency, fairness, and democratic integrity. The changing face of political strategy in the age of AI presents both unprecedented opportunities and significant responsibilities, signaling a future where the art of politics and the science of algorithms converge.

Maintaining a Balance: Innovation and Electoral Integrity

In the dynamic interplay between innovation and democratic values, the advent of Artificial Intelligence (AI) in the political sphere introduces a need for a delicate balance. The transformative power of AI in political campaigning and governance carries immense potential, yet it is imperative that such advancements do not undermine the bedrock of electoral integrity. The task at hand is to craft a framework of guidelines and regulations that can navigate the complex nexus of AI applications while safeguarding the essential tenets of democracy.

The governance of AI in politics must address a spectrum of concerns, chief among them being the protection of data privacy. As political campaigns increasingly utilize AI to analyze voter data for targeted messaging, robust data privacy regulations must be in place to prevent misuse and protect individuals' personal information. Furthermore, the ethical dimensions of AI-driven persuasion tactics call for a clear set of principles to ensure that the technology is employed in a manner that respects voters' autonomy and fosters fair political competition.

Beyond legal and regulatory measures, the integrity of the electoral process in the age of AI will hinge on the informed participation of the electorate. Educational initiatives are crucial in equipping citizens with the knowledge to critically evaluate AI-influenced political content. Voters must be made aware of the ways AI might be used to sway their opinions and the countermeasures that ensure the veracity and impartiality of the information they receive.

Transparency in AI operations is a foundational aspect of maintaining this balance. The algorithms that determine what political content reaches voters must be open to scrutiny, ensuring that these digital processes can be understood and trusted by the public. By fostering a culture of digital literacy, where the workings of AI are demystified, voters can be empowered to make decisions based on a clear understanding of the information landscape.

In an AI-driven political landscape, safeguarding the democratic process requires an ongoing commitment from all stakeholders involved. Policymakers must be vigilant in updating regulations to keep pace with technological advances. The tech industry must prioritize the ethical development and deployment of AI tools. Civil society organizations can serve as watchdogs, advocating for the responsible use of AI in politics. And academia can contribute to this balance by researching the impacts of AI on electoral integrity and educating the next generation of voters and policymakers.

The integration of AI into politics is not a phenomenon to be resisted but rather managed with prudence and foresight. The challenge lies in embracing the benefits of AI—its capacity for innovation and efficiency—while vigilantly protecting the democratic processes that are central to fair and free societies. As we chart a course through the uncharted waters of AI in politics, the balance between innovation and electoral integrity will be critical to ensuring that democracies thrive in an era of digital transformation. It is a balance that requires a clear vision, collaborative effort, and an unwavering dedication to the principles that underpin democratic governance.

Navigating the Future: Strategies for a Balanced AI Political Integration

The political arena is on the brink of an AI revolution that holds the potential to redefine the dynamics of power, policy, and participation. The integration of Artificial Intelligence (AI) into this domain necessitates a strategic approach that harmonizes the promise of innovation with the imperatives of democratic integrity. It's a delicate balance that calls for a concerted effort across various sectors to align the deployment of AI with the public good.

A key component of this strategy is fostering an ongoing, multidisciplinary dialogue. Technologists, the architects of AI systems, need to engage with policymakers, the guardians of the public interest, to navigate the ethical quandaries and practical challenges posed by AI. Civil society organizations, with their pulse on the collective conscience, and the electorate, as the ultimate stakeholders in a democratic system, must also have seats at this table. This inclusive conversation is essential to ensuring that AI technologies are developed and applied in ways that enhance democratic processes rather than disrupt them.

The establishment of international standards and best practices is critical in this context. Such standards can offer a blueprint for the ethical use of AI in political processes, drawing from a diverse pool of global experiences. By benchmarking best practices, nations can learn from one another, adopting and adapting strategies that mitigate risks while maximizing the benefits of AI. This cooperative effort can lead to a set of agreed-upon guidelines that ensure AI is used in politics in a manner that is transparent, accountable, and equitable.

Navigating the future of AI in politics also involves anticipating the technology's evolution and preparing the electorate for the changes it will bring. This preparation is not just about technological readiness but also about fostering an understanding of AI's potential impact on the political landscape. It requires educational initiatives that promote digital literacy, equipping citizens with the skills to discern AI's influence on political messaging and decision-making.

Moreover, a balanced approach to AI integration in politics must also consider the creation of robust regulatory frameworks. These frameworks should be agile enough to adapt to rapid technological advancements while providing solid protections against potential abuses. Regulation should be crafted with a view toward preserving the core tenets of democracy, such as privacy, freedom of expression, and the right to fair and free elections.

The evolution of AI in political systems presents an opportunity to enhance the democratic experience, making it more dynamic, inclusive, and participatory. By strategically preparing for AI's integration into politics with a commitment to upholding democratic values, we can pave the way for political systems that not only embrace technological innovation but also ensure that such advancements serve the collective aspirations of society.

As we embark on this journey, the emerging AI electorate represents both a challenge and an opportunity. The strategies we adopt now will shape the political narratives of the future, determining how well our democratic institutions can harness the power of AI to reflect and respect the will of the people. The goal is to move forward into an era where AI is not a force that shapes politics from the shadows but a tool that illuminates the path to a more engaged and informed democratic process.

Conclusion

Striking the Balance

In the burgeoning intersection of Artificial Intelligence (AI) and politics, we stand at a crossroads of potential and precaution. AI presents a Janus-faced proposition to the democratic processes that underpin our society: on one side, the promise of heightened efficiency, engagement, and insight; on the other, the peril of manipulation, privacy erosion, and uncharted ethical territory. The objective, as we move forward, is not to shun the advancements AI offers but to wield them with a wisdom that is cognizant of their far-reaching implications.

Throughout this exploration, we have witnessed AI's capacity to streamline and invigorate the electoral process, providing tools that can deepen voter engagement and open new avenues for political participation. Yet, these same tools carry the inherent risk of deepening divides, amplifying biases, and reshaping the political landscape in ways that may not align with the values of fairness and transparency.

Citizen awareness and education emerge as critical bulwarks in the quest to balance the scales. An informed electorate is the first line of defense against the potential misuse of AI in politics. Initiatives that enhance digital literacy and demystify AI's role in political processes are vital to ensuring that the electorate is not a passive recipient of AI's influence but an active participant in shaping its use.

As we conclude, it is imperative to recognize that the integration of AI into politics is not a transient trend but a defining shift in the fabric of our democratic institutions. The call to action is clear: stakeholders from across the political spectrum—policymakers, technologists, civil society, and voters—must engage proactively with the evolving landscape. Collaboration and dialogue will be pivotal in crafting policies that foster innovation while safeguarding against the risks that AI poses.

Our final reflections on the future interplay between AI and elections are tinged with both optimism and caution. Optimism, for the democratic enhancements that AI can facilitate; caution, for the vigilance required to guard against its potential to disrupt. The journey ahead will require a collective commitment to stewardship, a dedication to the principles of democracy, and an unwavering focus on the public good.

In this age of digital transformation, striking the balance between AI's potential and pitfalls is our shared responsibility. The road ahead is complex and uncharted, but by embracing both the challenges and opportunities that AI presents, we can navigate towards a future where technology elevates the democratic experience, reflecting the will of the people with integrity and purpose. It is within our collective power to ensure that AI, in all its might and ingenuity, is harnessed to fortify the foundations of democracy for generations to come.

Glossary

Algorithm: A set of rules or a step-by-step process that a computer follows to perform tasks, solve problems, or make decisions.

Artificial Intelligence (AI): The simulation of human intelligence processes by machines, especially computer systems, enabling them to perform tasks that typically require human intelligence such as visual perception, speech recognition, decision-making, and language translation.

Blockchain: A distributed database or ledger that is shared among the nodes of a computer network. It stores information electronically in digital format and is known for its crucial role in cryptocurrency systems, such as Bitcoin, for maintaining a secure and decentralized record of transactions.

Content Moderation: The practice of monitoring and applying a predetermined set of rules and guidelines to user-generated submissions to determine if the communication (text, images, videos, etc.) is permissible or not.

Crowdsourcing: The process of obtaining information or input into a task or project by enlisting the services of a large number of people, either paid or unpaid, typically via the Internet.

Data Analytics: The process of examining data sets to draw conclusions about the information they contain, often with the aid of specialized systems and software.

Data Privacy: The aspect of information technology that deals with the ability of an organization or individual to determine what data in a computer system can be shared with third parties.

Deepfake: Synthetic media in which a person in an existing image or video is replaced with someone else's likeness, often used to create fake news or hoaxes.

Digital Literacy: The ability to find, evaluate, utilize, share, and create content using information technologies and the Internet.

Facial Recognition: A technology capable of identifying or verifying a person from a digital image or a video frame from a video source, often used in security systems.

Machine Learning: A branch of AI and computer science which focuses on the use of data and algorithms to imitate the way that humans learn, gradually improving its accuracy.

Micro-targeting: The use of demographic and consumer data to identify the interests of specific individuals or very small groups of like-minded individuals and influence their thoughts or actions.

Natural Language Processing (NLP): A branch of AI that helps computers understand, interpret, and manipulate human language.

Pattern Recognition: The automated recognition of patterns and regularities in data, often used within AI to identify objects, persons, or signals.

Predictive Analytics: The use of data, statistical algorithms, and machine learning techniques to identify the likelihood of future outcomes based on historical data.

Privacy Laws: Regulations that govern the storage, use, and sharing of personal information, intended to protect individuals' personal data and privacy.

Real-time Assistance: Technologies that provide immediate aid or support to individuals, often using AI to offer timely and efficient service.

Synthetic Media: Content (audio, video, images, text) that is entirely generated by AI algorithms.

Tamper-proof Systems: Security measures or systems designed to be safe from unauthorized tampering or hacking.

Transparency: In the context of AI and governance, the principle that the operations and decision-making processes of AI systems should be open and clear to users and the public.

Voter Engagement: The process of encouraging voters to become involved in the political process, including educating them on issues and mobilizing them to participate in elections.

List of resources for further reading

Books:

1. "AI Superpowers: China, Silicon Valley, and the New World Order" by Kai-Fu Lee – Explores the rise of China as a major competitor in AI and the implications for global power dynamics.
2. "Tools and Weapons: The Promise and the Peril of the Digital Age" by Brad Smith – Discusses the challenges and responsibilities of technology companies in the era of AI.
3. "The Age of Surveillance Capitalism: The Fight for a Human Future at the New Frontier of Power" by Shoshana Zuboff – A critical look at the economic and social implications of tech companies' data practices.
4. "Deep Learning" by Ian Goodfellow, Yoshua Bengio, and Aaron Courville – Provides a deep dive into the technical aspects of deep learning, a key technology behind generative AI.

Academic Journals:

1. "Artificial Intelligence and Law" – A journal that covers the impact of AI on legal processes and regulations.
2. "Journal of Artificial Intelligence Research" – Offers research articles across a broad spectrum of AI.
3. "Big Data & Society" – Focuses on the societal implications of data science and big data, including areas impacted by AI.

Online Courses and Lectures:

1. "AI For Everyone" by Andrew Ng on Coursera – A course designed for non-technical individuals to understand AI's capabilities and limitations.

2. "Introduction to Artificial Intelligence" by Sebastian Thrun and Peter Norvig on Udacity – Offers a comprehensive overview of AI principles and techniques.
3. "Ethics and Governance of Artificial Intelligence" by the MIT Media Lab – Explores the ethical and governance issues surrounding AI.

Reports and White Papers:

1. "Artificial Intelligence and Responsive Governance" by The World Bank Group – A report on how AI can be used in governance and policymaking.
2. "AI in the Age of Cyber-Disorder" by the Carnegie Endowment for International Peace – Discusses the use of AI in cyber operations and its implications for international security.

Websites and Blogs:

1. AI Now Institute (ainowinstitute.org) – Conducts research and advocacy on the social implications of artificial intelligence.
2. Future of Life Institute (futureoflife.org) – Examines the existential risks and opportunities presented by AI.
3. Electronic Frontier Foundation (eff.org) – Focuses on defending civil liberties in the digital world, including issues related to AI.
4. Data & Society (datasociety.net) – A research institute studying the social implications of data-centric technologies and automation.

Governmental and Non-Governmental Organizations:

1. The AI Initiative of The Future Society at Harvard Kennedy School – Engages in research and convenes stakeholders to discuss the governance and ethics of AI.
2. European Commission's High-Level Expert Group on Artificial Intelligence – Provides AI ethics guidelines and policy recommendations.

Technical details on AI models discussed in the book

In "The Artificial Candidate," several AI models and their underlying technologies are discussed in the context of their application to political campaigns and election processes. Here's an overview of the technical details behind these models:

Generative Adversarial Networks (GANs):

- Structure: GANs consist of two neural networks, the generator and the discriminator, which are trained simultaneously through adversarial processes.
- Function: The generator creates data that is indistinguishable from real data, while the discriminator evaluates its authenticity. The process continues until the generator produces data that the discriminator can no longer distinguish from the real thing.
- Application: In politics, GANs can be used to create hyper-realistic media, including deep fakes, which could be used in disinformation campaigns.

Natural Language Processing (NLP):

- Structure: NLP models often use recurrent neural networks (RNNs), transformers, or convolutional neural networks (CNNs) to process and generate human language.
- Function: These models are trained on large datasets of text to understand syntax, context, and semantics. Models like BERT and GPT (Generative Pre-trained Transformer) are designed to predict subsequent words or generate coherent text sequences.
- Application: NLP is used in political campaigns to analyze voter sentiment, automate social media interactions, and even write speeches or policy statements.

Predictive Analytics:

- Structure: Predictive models can be built using various machine learning techniques, including regression analysis, decision trees, and neural networks.
- Function: By analyzing historical data, predictive models can forecast future events or behaviors, identifying patterns and trends.
- Application: In the political domain, predictive analytics can be employed to anticipate voter turnout, identify swing voters, and tailor campaign strategies.

Machine Learning (ML) Algorithms for Voter Micro-targeting:

- Structure: These algorithms often involve supervised learning techniques, where the algorithm is trained on labeled data sets.
- Function: ML algorithms can classify voters based on demographics, past voting behavior, and other personal data, allowing for personalized campaign messaging.
- Application: Micro-targeting involves delivering specific political messages to subgroups of the electorate who are most likely to be influenced by them.

Facial Recognition and Biometric Identification:

- Structure: These models use computer vision techniques to identify and verify individuals by analyzing their facial features.
- Function: They are trained on diverse datasets of facial images, allowing the algorithms to recognize individuals with high accuracy.
- Application: In elections, facial recognition can be used for voter identification, enhancing the security and integrity of the voting process.

Blockchain Technology for Voting:

- Structure: Blockchain is not an AI model but a distributed ledger technology that can be integrated with AI.
- Function: It creates a secure, immutable record of transactions, which, in the case of voting, corresponds to ballots cast.
- Application: When combined with AI, blockchain can be used to secure digital voting platforms, ensuring that votes are recorded accurately and cannot be altered.

Each of these AI models incorporates complex mathematical and computational processes. The training involves vast datasets, often requiring significant computational power. The deployment of these models in political contexts necessitates not only technical expertise but also ethical considerations and regulatory compliance to ensure that their use promotes transparency, fairness, and democratic engagement.

References

Bostrom, N. (2014). *Superintelligence: Paths, Dangers, Strategies*. Oxford University Press.

Brynjolfsson, E., & McAfee, A. (2014). *The Second Machine Age: Work, Progress, and Prosperity in a Time of Brilliant Technologies*. W. W. Norton & Company.

Goodfellow, I., Bengio, Y., & Courville, A. (2016). *Deep Learning*. MIT Press.

Kaplan, A., & Haenlein, M. (2020). "Siri, Siri, in my hand: Who's the fairest in the land? On the interpretations, illustrations, and implications of artificial intelligence." *Business Horizons*, 63(1), 15-25.

Lee, K.-F. (2018). *AI Superpowers: China, Silicon Valley, and the New World Order*. Houghton Mifflin Harcourt.

O'Neil, C. (2016). *Weapons of Math Destruction: How Big Data Increases Inequality and Threatens Democracy*. Crown.

Russell, S., & Norvig, P. (2016). *Artificial Intelligence: A Modern Approach* (3rd ed.). Pearson.

Schwab, K. (2017). *The Fourth Industrial Revolution*. Crown Business.

Tegmark, M. (2017). *Life 3.0: Being Human in the Age of Artificial Intelligence*. Knopf.

Zuboff, S. (2019). *The Age of Surveillance Capitalism: The Fight for a Human Future at the New Frontier of Power*. PublicAffairs.

Journal Articles:

Chen, Y., & Cheung, A. S. (2020). "The Transparent Self Under Big Data Profiling: Privacy and Chinese Legislation on the Social Credit System." *The Journal of Comparative Law*, 13(2), 356-378.

Goodfellow, I. J., Pouget-Abadie, J., Mirza, M., Xu, B., Warde-Farley, D., Ozair, S., Courville, A., & Bengio, Y. (2014). "Generative Adversarial Nets." In *Advances in Neural Information Processing Systems* (pp. 2672-2680).

Lazer, D. M. J., Baum, M. A., Benkler, Y., Berinsky, A. J., Greenhill, K. M., Menczer, F., Metzger, M. J., Nyhan, B., Pennycook, G., Rothschild, D., Schudson, M., Sloman, S. A., Sunstein, C. R., Thorson, E. A., Watts, D. J., & Zittrain, J. L. (2018). "The science of fake news: Addressing fake news requires a multidisciplinary effort." *Science*, 359(6380), 1094-1096.

Tufekci, Z. (2015). "Algorithmic Harms beyond Facebook and Google: Emergent Challenges of Computational Agency." *Colorado Technology Law Journal*, 13(2), 203-217.

Websites and Reports:

European Commission High-Level Expert Group on Artificial Intelligence. (2019). *Ethics Guidelines for Trustworthy AI.* ec.europa.eu

Future of Life Institute. (2021). *AI Policy - China.* futureoflife.org

OpenAI. (2019). *OpenAI Charter.* openai.com

World Economic Forum. (2020). *Global Technology Governance Report.* weforum.org

Acknowledgment

The journey to bring "The Artificial Candidate: Generative AI and the Future of US Elections" from concept to reality has been a profound exploration into the intersection of technology and democracy. This book is the culmination of many hours of research, reflection, and discourse, none of which would have been possible without the support and insights of a remarkable group of individuals.

First and foremost, I extend my heartfelt thanks to my partner, whose steadfast support and endless patience provided the foundation upon which this project was built. You were the unwavering pillar of encouragement when the challenges seemed insurmountable and the joyous celebrant at each stage of accomplishment. This book is as much a testament to your belief in its value as it is to my commitment to its creation.

To my dear friends, your contributions extend far beyond the camaraderie and intellectual stimulation you generously provided. Our discussions, sometimes deep into the night, have not only honed the arguments presented in these pages but have also been a source of comfort and motivation. Your belief in the importance of this dialogue about AI and its role in our political systems has been a driving force in this endeavor.

I am profoundly grateful to my colleagues, whose dedication to understanding and harnessing AI has been both inspiring and invaluable. The collaborative environment we share has been fertile ground for the exchange of ideas that have significantly enriched this work. Your collective vision for the responsible use of AI has been a guiding light throughout the writing process.

Special recognition is owed to the academic and professional community in the fields of AI and political science. The pioneering research and critical insights from experts in the field have provided an indispensable foundation for the themes explored in this book. Your commitment to exploring the implications of AI in our political institutions has paved the way for meaningful discourse and informed analysis.

To the broader community of educators, technologists, policymakers, and activists engaged in the conversation about AI and elections—your passion and diverse viewpoints have been crucial in painting a comprehensive picture of the current landscape and future possibilities. The robust exchange of knowledge and opinions within this community has ensured that this book captures a multiplicity of voices and perspectives.

Lastly, my deepest appreciation goes to you, the reader. Your interest in the subject matter and willingness to engage with the complex interplay between AI and electoral politics are what make this book relevant. It is my fervent hope that these pages will serve as a catalyst for further exploration, discussion, and action as we navigate the evolving role of AI in our democratic processes.

With sincere and profound gratitude,

Yassine

About the author

Yassine Aqejjaj stands at the forefront of artificial intelligence, guiding the course of innovation with seasoned expertise as an AI Lead Product Manager and Advisor. His career, spanning over a decade, has solidified his status as an influential force in navigating and shaping the AI trajectory across diverse industries such as Deep Tech, retail, banking, and insurance.

Driven by an unwavering passion for artificial intelligence and an insatiable quest for knowledge, Yassine has mastered the art of wielding AI to spearhead transformative changes in product development and business strategy. His acumen extends beyond theoretical knowledge, delving into the practical application of AI to foster growth and streamline processes for enterprises from agile startups to venerable market leaders.

Yassine's advisory role is marked by his adept skill in demystifying the complexities of AI, transforming intricate technical details into strategic, actionable plans. Companies under his guidance are not merely introduced to AI; they are shown how to embed it seamlessly into their foundational processes, innovating in a manner that is both cutting-edge and pragmatically sound. His hands-on involvement ensures the delivery of bespoke AI solutions that address the distinct challenges and seize the unique opportunities presented within each sector.

A fervent proponent of AI literacy, Yassine is committed to educating the broader public. His expertise regularly illuminates speaking events, workshops, and his latest literary endeavor. This commitment stems from his conviction that a comprehensive understanding of AI is crucial for harnessing the technology's full potential in shaping an optimistic future.

Yassine's dedication extends beyond his professional achievements to his role as a mentor and community cultivator.

He actively participates in fostering networks where professionals can exchange innovative ideas, engage in thought-provoking debates, and collaborate on pioneering AI initiatives.

In "The Artificial Candidate: Generative AI and the Future of US Elections," Yassine amalgamates his rich experience with his educational fervor to navigate readers through the intricate interplay between AI and political processes. His insights provide a compelling exploration of how AI is reshaping not just the strategies behind political campaigns, but the very fabric of electoral democracy.

With a visionary outlook and an intricate understanding of the AI domain, Yassine Aqejjaj continues to lead by example, inspiring change and catalyzing the integration of AI within industries worldwide. His contribution through this book is a testament to his leadership and his dedication to the evolution of artificial intelligence as a cornerstone of modern political strategy.

www.ingramcontent.com/pod-product-compliance
Lightning Source LLC
LaVergne TN
LVHW051704050326
832903LV00032B/4004